Other geeky titles by D. Michael Parrish:

Development of a Tidal Constituent Database for the St. Johns River Water Management District

Target Element Sizes for Finite Element Tidal Models from a Domain-Wide, Localized Truncation Error Analysis Incorporating Bottom Stress and Coriolis Force

C is for Children

My First Thirty-Two Keywords

D. MICHAEL PARRISH

**Illustrated by
D. Michael, Denwood M.,
Lottie M., and Edward J. Parrish**

iUniverse LLC
Bloomington

C IS FOR CHILDREN
My First Thirty-Two Keywords

Copyright © 2014 D. Michael Parrish

All rights reserved. No part of this book may be used or reproduced by any means, graphic, electronic, or mechanical, including photocopying, recording, taping or by any information storage retrieval system without the written permission of the publisher except in the case of brief quotations embodied in critical articles and reviews.

iUniverse books may be ordered through booksellers or by contacting:

iUniverse LLC
1663 Liberty Drive
Bloomington, IN 47403
www.iuniverse.com
1-800-Authors (1-800-288-4677)

Because of the dynamic nature of the Internet, any web addresses or links contained in this book may have changed since publication and may no longer be valid. The views expressed in this work are solely those of the author and do not necessarily reflect the views of the publisher, and the publisher hereby disclaims any responsibility for them.

ISBN: 978-1-4917-1359-4 (sc)
ISBN: 978-1-4917-1360-0 (e)

Library of Congress Control Number: 2013921272

Printed in the United States of America.

iUniverse rev. date: 01/17/2014

The epigraph is taken from the Holy Bible (Textus Receptus and King James Version).

Cover art background image copyright Moya Phototography, Inc. Used with permission.

CONTENTS

LIST OF TABLES

LIST OF FIGURES

LIST OF PROGRAMS

for Denwood, Lottie, and Edward

Εν αρχή ην ο λόγος
In the beginning was the Word

NOTE TO PARENTS
AND GUARDIANS

I've picked up a few programming languages over the years: I use them in my work as an engineer as well as in my play time. Last summer my wife asked me to teach our kids how to program computers. I did not find a children's book on C, so I thought I would write one and publish it so that you and your children could benefit from the effort I've already put in.

Why should kids learn to program computers? Computer programming is exercise for the mind. Computer programming is a valuable, if not essential skill for many professions. If you live in the United States, it can be more important than fluency in a human language other than English. I have used the French I learned in high school very little, and don't know Spanish, even though I have lived in Florida and northern Virginia for decades, where Spanish is fairly common. Much of the work I do as an engineer could not be done, or could not be done very quickly, without some programming. Just as with human languages, it is never too early to begin learning computer languages. I began at about age seven, just as Commodore was getting low-cost personal computers into our living rooms.

I think C is a good first computer language. Many other computer languages are based on C, and many languages not based on C include concepts inherent to C. Also, the C89 standard has only 32 keywords—convenient for a brief introductory text such as the one you are reading now.

Although this is a book for children (grade 3 or so), I hope that you will assist your child with the new words that are printed in emphasized text, and which are all defined herein. I hope you will also assist your child reader with the exercises by doing some typing and / or copying and pasting from the website, tiny.cc/cisforchildren.

This book begins introducing C with nothing (almost literally). If your child reads English at about the 3rd grade level, he or she should be able to read this book, and should expect to see about three new words per page. It will help if the child reader has a sense of numbers and an arithmetic ability normally acquired by about grade 3 (e.g., counting rules, addition, subtraction, awareness of negative numbers and fractions). The computer will do the math, but it will help to have an idea of what is going on.

Neither you nor your child need to know how to type in order to learn C. Hunt-and-peck works just fine. My high-school computer programming teacher did not know how to type—and neither did I at the time—but what I learned in that class earned me college credit through an Advanced Placement Computer Science exam. As a beginning programmer, you do a lot more work with your brain than with your fingers.

I hope you will have a C compiler installed on your computer so that you can try the example programs along with any of your own. If you are new to C, you might start with gcc or MinGW (basic instructions on how to obtain MinGW are provided in the Appendix).

This book reflects the C89 standard. Keywords added by subsequent standards are not discussed.

I have been inspired by a book that Professor Scott C. Hagen gave me to read in about 2000 A.D., called *Just Enough Unix*. By the way, congratulations, Scott, on having achieved the rank of full professor in 2012.

My children (2nd and 3rd graders) have read through a draft of this book with the kind of assistance I mentioned above. They were paid $0.25 per lesson for their review comments, many of which are reflected in this version.

If you find errors in this book or have specific questions about the content, please send e-mail to cisforchildren@yahoo.com. If you provide corrections or material that I use in a subsequent edition, I will—if you request it, and if space allows—acknowledge you therein.

The book's website is http://pegasus.cc.ucf.edu/~dparrish/ c4k_main.htm (you can also use tinyurl.com/cisforchildren or tiny.cc/cisforchildren. At the website, you may find electronic versions of the programs in this book, corrections, and other items of interest.

ACKNOWLEDGEMENTS

Thank you, Denwood, Lottie, and Edward for providing the impetus for this book. And thank you for being my first readers and reviewers. You know who `else` reviewed this book? My mom!

—Daddy 8-)

Mom, thank you very much for reviewing this book and for all your input and output.

—Michael

INTRODUCTION

I once read a book about football.

What's that? You thought this was a book about computers? It is. But I want those who know very little to be able to read this book. So, we'll start with something the reader knows about.

As I said, I once read a book about football. I learned the rules of football. But, I did not become a great football player. You have to do more than read a book about football to become a great football player. You have to play the game. But, you will not become a great football player if you do not know the rules.

This book will begin to teach you the rules of **C**. C is a code that you can use to tell your computer what to do. You say C like the word "see." You need to do more than read this book to become good at C. But you must know most of the things in this book in order to do useful things with C. To become good at C, you must practice using it. You can start by doing the exercises in this book.

How To Read this Book:

This book has some stuff that might be new to you. This section tells you about that stuff.

This book is made up of parts and chapters. Each part has chapters that go together. Each chapter has one topic or a few topics that go together.

Each part or chapter begins on a new page. There are guidewords on the top-outside corners of many pages. The guidewords tell you what part of C those pages are about.

Chapters may have labeled sections. The section you are reading now is labeled "How To Read this Book." Section labels have a colon (:) on the right side. They have a blank line above and below.

When I talk about a punctuation mark, I may show that mark nearby. I did that in the last paragraph when I used the word "colon."

Speaking of punctuation marks, I use the apostrophe (') in a way that you may not have seen before. I use it to make some plurals. Remember, a plural is a word that means more than one of something. The plural of "cat" is "cats." Just add an "s." But, sometimes adding an "s" can be confusing. What is the plural of A, as in the letter A? Is it As? Hmm. As looks like the word "as." If just adding an "s" might confuse you, I put an apostrophe before the "s." So, the plural of R is R's, and the plural of 5 is 5's. I also make the plural of keywords with an apostrophe before the "s."

Some parts and chapters start with short statements, quotes, poems, or dialogues. These are meant to be funny or interesting or curious.

This book writes letters in different ways for different reasons. Some words or groups of words are written using letters that look like *this* (*itallics*), so that they stand out.

New words look like **this** (**boldface**). Except, you already know the word "this." ☺ When I use a new word, I will tell you what it means. The glossary will also tell you what it means. Sometimes, I will tell you how to say a new word. I will use the ear symbol 𝔇 "sim bol" with some letters in double quotes, "". Those letters will have a clue about how to say the new word. The clues may not tell you *exactly* how to say the word, but they will point you in the right direction.

C code is written like `this`. In `code`, each letter has the same width as the others, and the letters are more like the ones you might write with a pencil than the ones you see in most books.

Each part of this book builds on the parts that come before it. Keep this in mind if you skip ahead.

This book begins counting at zero because C starts counting at zero.

PART 0

Much Ado about Nothing

In this part, you will learn how to tell your computer to keep track of things. The theme of this part is *nothing* (see Figure 0). The word "nothing" can mean "not important," but in C, *nothing* is *very* important. That is why this book starts with *nothing*.

Figure 0: Nothing

```
/* notes */
```

CHAPTER 0

Nothing

> "Near my home there used to be a beautiful lake, but then it was gone."
>
> "Did the lake dry up?"
>
> "No, it just wasn't there anymore. Nothing was there anymore. Not even a dried up lake."
>
> "A hole?"
>
> "No, a hole would *be* something . . . it was *nothing*."
>
> —Petersen and Weigel, *The Neverending Story*

You can use English to tell stories. You can use C to write directions for computers, called **programs**. Stories are made of sentences, and programs are made of statements.

The simplest statement is

;

(a **semicolon**). This is called a **null statement**. "Null" means "nothing." The null statement means "do nothing." All statements must end in a semicolon. A null statement has a semicolon, the whole semicolon, and *nothing* but the semicolon. A null statement is nothing, followed by a semicolon.

Nothing does a good job in a null statement. But, sometimes, you need *something* to stand for *nothing*. When I talk, I use the word "nothing" to stand for *nothing*. So does Buttercup:

> "Is there a village nearby?" asked Vizzini.
> "There is *nothing* nearby," replied Buttercup.
>
> —William Goldman, *The Princess Bride*

In C, the keyword `void` stands for *nothing*. If you guessed that "void" means "nothing," you guessed right.

Exercise:

(As this chapter is about *nothing*, there are *no* exercises.)

Summary:

You have learned *something* about *nothing*, but not *everything*.

CHAPTER 1

Anything, Anywhere, and Nowhere

"Where are you going?"
"Looks like I'm going nowhere."

—George Lucas, *Star Wars Episode IV*

Sometimes, you need to know where something is. Your house has an address. The address tells where your house is. In C, an **address** is something that tells where some part of your program is. Addresses are also called **pointers** because they point to something (like the hands in Figure 1).

In the last chapter, you learned that the keyword void stands for *nothing*. If you want your computer to keep track of where *anything* is,

---

He made a molten sea of ten *cubits from brim to brim, round in compass . . .* thirty *cubits did compass it round about.*

3   3.1415926535897932

Figure 1: Hands pointing: *left* to the number 3, *up* to some text, *nowhere*, *down* to another number, and *right* to a circle.

you could use the keyword `void` together with a **star**. For example, you could use the statement:

<code>void * anywhere;</code>

In this statement, `anywhere` is a **name**. That statement tells the computer to make a pointer called `anywhere`. If you give that statement to your computer, you are telling it that `anywhere` is a certain place in your computer. That place could be anywhere in your computer—any *possible* place—not on the moon! That place could be anywhere because you have not told it where. *What* is at `anywhere`? You won't know unless you put something there or ask the computer to tell you what's there. The `anywhere` pointer *could* point to the sequence of letters and punctuation marks from Carroll's poem—and, no, I *don't* expect you to read it:

```
'Twas brillig, and the slithy toves\nDid gyre and
gimble in the wabe:\nAll mimsy were the borogoves,\
nAnd the mome raths outgrabe.\n
```

When you tell the computer to make a pointer, you can also tell it to make the pointer point *nowhere*, like this:

<code>void * nowhere = (void *)0;</code>

The stuff on the left side of the equals sign tells the computer to make a pointer. The equals sign tells the computer that you are going to tell it where the pointer should point. The stuff on the right side tells the computer where the pointer should point; `(void *)0` means *nowhere*.

In this case, `nowhere` is a name that means *nowhere* because the stuff on the right side of the equals sign means *nowhere*.

In your computer, everything is somewhere. The only thing that can be *nowhere* is *nothing*. Now, `nowhere` *is* somewhere. But `nowhere` *points* nowhere. You could also say that `nowhere` points to *nothing*.

You can name anything. In this chapter, you have already seen how to name pointers. Names let you tell the computer what to do with the things that have those names. Without names, you can't write even one C program. Some other examples of names you can use in your C programs are `main`, `Thing1`, and `George`. You can name the things you make *almost* anything. But names must follow these rules:

0. Names *must* begin with a letter of the English alphabet or the **underscore, _**.
1. Names may have English letters, the underscore, and the digits 0, 1, 2, 3, 4, 5, 6, 7, 8, and 9 *only*.
2. Names *should* be *shorter* than 32 letters, digits, and underscores.

(See Figure 2.) These rules won't let you make the name `John Jacob Jingleheimer Schmidt`, but the rules *will* let you make the names `JohnJacobJingleheimerSchmidt` and `John_Jacob_Jingleheimer_Schmidt`. Your program might not do what you want if you try to use both `John_Jacob_Jingleheimer_Schmidt1` and `John_Jacob_Jingleheimer_Schmidt2` because they each have the same first 31 letters, digits, and underscores. The computer *may* ignore the 1 and the 2 at the end of the names. Then the two names will look the same. `John_Jacob_Jingleheimer_Schmidt1` might think, "`John_Jacob_Jingleheimer_Schmidt`! His name is my name, too!"

You have a lot of freedom when you make names. Use that freedom wisely. I think you should use names that are "as simple as possible, but not simpler." That's what Einstein said about everything. If you are naming a *thing*, use a noun. If you are naming an *action*, use a verb.

The Alphbet

```
_ 0 1 2 3 4 5 6 7
8 9 A C B D E F G
H I J K L M N O P
Q R S T U V W X Y
Z a b c d e f g h
i j k l m n o p q
r s t u v w x y z
```

Figure 2: What's in a Name. Names may have the underscore, digits, and English letters.

```
void *
```

CHAPTER 2

Something

You have learned about *nothing, anything, anywhere,* and *nowhere.* Now, you will learn about *something.*

Sometimes, you need a *number* that means "nothing." That number is zero. Zero *is* something, even though its **value** means "nothing." At the same time, the number is not just *anything* (it is not Hogwarts School of Witchcraft and Wizardry, for example). It is a *number.*

In the last chapter, you learned that the keyword `void` stands for *nothing.* The keyword `int` 👂 rhymes with "hint," stands for a number.

The keyword `int` comes from "**integer.**" The integers are 0, 1, -1, 2, -2, 3, -3, and so on. In math, the integers go on forever. In C, an `int` can hold any integer from as high as 32,767 to as low as -32,767. We say that an `int` can **range** from -32,767 to 32,767.

An `int` *might* be able to hold numbers less than -32,767 or greater than 32,767, but this depends on your computer, your operating system (such as Linux or Windows), and your **compiler** 👂 "come pile er."

A compiler reads your C code and writes instructions for your computer called **machine code**. Those instructions have the same meaning as your C code. No, your computer does not understand C, but you do—or you will. And you do not understand machine code, but your computer does. Yes, you use one program to make another program. (One of my teachers used English to teach French.) In this book, I call the combination of the computer, the operating system, and the compiler, the "**system.**" In another book "system" might mean something else.

9

`int`

You can tell the computer to remember a number by using the keyword `int`. For example, you could use the statement:

```
int an_integer = 0;
```

In the above example, `an_integer` is a name, and the statement says to make an `int` called `an_integer`, then give it the value zero.

CHAPTER 3

Statement

So far, you have seen three examples of statements:

```
          ;
void * anywhere;
int an_integer = 0;
```

Statements are made from four kinds of things. You have already seen examples of each. First are *symbols* like the semicolon (;), the star (*), and the equals sign (=). Second are *keywords*, for example, void and int. Third are *names*, like anything and an_integer. Finally, statements may contain *values*, like 0.

/* notes */

CHAPTER 4

Return of Nothing, Definition of Nothing

"Nothing comes from nothing."

—Parmenides

All programs have at least one **function** 👂 "funk shun." Functions tell the computer what to do, and *in what order*. Functions have four parts: a name, input, a process, and output.

Functions are like pets. You call them by their names, you feed them certain kinds of input, and they process it. The input gets "chewed" and "digested." Then, stuff comes out. As with pets, some functions are already named. If *you* make a function, you will give it a name. Functions can be picky eaters or can be made to eat almost anything. Each function outputs or **returns** only one kind, or **type**, of thing, called the **return type**.

You can also think of the parts of a function like this:

0. what it *gives* (output),
1. what it is *called* (name),
2. what it *gets* (input), and
3. what it *does* (process).

Every function should contain a `return` statement. For example, we could make, or **define** a `nothing` function:

```
void nothing (void) {return;}
```

13

The first part of a **function definition** tells what type of thing the function *gives*. The first thing in the definition of nothing is the keyword void. So, nothing returns void, or *nothing*.

The second part of a function definition tells what the function is *called* or named. The second thing in the definition of nothing is the name nothing. Therefore, the function is called nothing.

The third part of a function definition tells what the function is *gets*. The third thing in the definition of nothing is a set of **parentheses** 👂 "puh ren thuh seas," () with the keyword void inside. Therefore, the function gets *nothing*. When you define a function, you *must* put parentheses after its name. Inside the parentheses, you must tell what the function gets.

The fourth part of a function definition tells what the function *does*. The fourth thing in the definition of nothing is a set of **braces** {} containing the statement

```
return;
```

This return statement is the only statement between the braces, so this is the only thing nothing does. There is nothing between the return keyword and the semicolon, so nothing returns *nothing*.

PART 1

Your First Program

Now that you know *something* about *nothing*, you have almost *everything* you need to write your first program. In this part of the book, you will see a complete program and explore the parts of that program.

/* notes */

CHAPTER 0

The `main` Idea

Every C program has a function called `main`. What does `main` do? It does what *you* tell it to do!

Doing what the program says to do is called **running** the program. When the computer runs your program, it begins with the statements that are outside of *any* function. Then, it will run `main`. This is like the way you do your homework. First, you read the directions at the top of the page. Then, you do problem 1, and so on.

The simplest program is:

```
int main (void) { return 0; }
```

I will call it Program Diddly Squat. (I thought about calling it Program Zero, but Program Diddly Squat is more fun.) Program Diddly Squat defines one function called `main`.

The definition of `main` begins with `int`, which is the return type. The `main` function returns an `int`. The next thing after `int` is the name of the function: `main`. The keyword `void` is between parentheses. So, `main` has no input. The `main` process begins at the **open brace**, {. The `main` function returns or outputs the value 0. The `main` process ends at the **close brace**, }.

When you type in Program Diddly Squat or any other program, use lower-case if lower-case is shown, and use upper-case if upper-case is shown. In C, the same letters written with different cases are different words! For example, `return` is a keyword, but `Return` and `RETURN` are not.

main

CHAPTER 1

Comment

You can add spaces and line breaks between keywords, names, symbols, and values. You can add space by pressing the space bar. And you can add a line break by pressing the Enter or Return key. Program Diddly Squat could have been written as on the next page.

Exercise:

0. In Program Diddly Squat, What type of thing does `main` give?
1. In Program Diddly Squat, What type of thing does `main` get?
2. In Program Diddly Squat, What does `main` do?
3. Enter, compile, and run Program Diddly Squat. From now on, I will say "try" instead of, "enter, compile, and run."

```
/*            Program Diddly Squat              */
/*                                             */
/* This is a comment. Comments go between a "slash */
/* star" and a "star slash." Your system will ig-  */
/* nore comments. You can use comments to explain  */
/* what your program does---or what you THINK it   */
/* does.                                           */
/*                                               */
/* On the next few lines, comments are used to ex- */
/* plain  main.                                  */
/*                                               */
   int      /* Part 1 tells the return type.    */
   main     /* Part 2 tells the name.           */
   (void)   /* Part 3 tells the input.          */
   {        /* Part 4 begins with {.            */
    return 0; /* Part 4 has one or more statements. */
   }        /* Part 4 ends with }.              */
/*                                               */
/* You can even use comments to include pictures in */
/* your  programs:                               */
/*                                               */
/*           ,88888.                           */
/*           8888888 [[[[[/                    */
/*           88/      [[[[[/                    */
/*           88                                 */
/*           88\      [[[[[\                    */
/*           8888888 [[[[[[\                    */
/*           '88888'                            */
/*                                               */
/*         End Program Diddly Squat             */
```

PART 2

The Three R's

"Two out of three ain't bad."

—unknown

So far, you have learned about the keywords `int`, `return`, and `void`. You have also learned about parentheses (), braces {}, and the semicolon (;).

Next, you will learn how to use functions so that you can make your computer read and write. That's two out of three R's (reading, writing, and arithmetic).

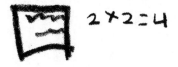

```
/* notes */
```

CHAPTER 0

Show Me

Sing me no song!
Read me no rhyme!
Don't waste my time!
Show me!

—Jay and Shaw, "Show Me," *My Fair Lady*

It's time to make your computer do something. You will use `printf` 𝔻 "print eff," which is a function, not a keyword. Most of the programs in this book use `printf`. The `printf` function lets you do **formatted** 𝔻 "for mat Ted" printing. A format tells *how* to print something. For example, the `printf` function lets you say where to start a new line. Here is an example `printf` statement:

```
printf("Hello, Nurse!");
```

The `printf` function sends the stuff between **double quotes**, `""`, to **standard output**. Standard output is almost always the computer screen, but it *could* be something else, like a printer. I am going to write "screen" instead of "standard output" from now on.

If you want to make your computer print something on the screen, you need to make a program like Program Hello Nurse:

```
printf
```

```
          /* Program Hello Nurse */

#include <stdio.h>

int main(void) {
    printf("Hello, Nurse!");
    return 0;
}

        /* End Program Hello Nurse */
```

The first line of Program Hello Nurse,

```
          #include <stdio.h>
```

This tells the computer to *include* some other stuff in our program. What other stuff? In this case, some stuff called `stdio.h` 👂 "standard eye oh." It defines `printf`. (The h in `stdio.h` stands for "**header**," meaning something at the **head**, or top.)

The `printf` function can do a lot more than put letters and words on the screen. You will find other ways to use `printf` in the rest of this book.

In this chapter, you have seen how to make the computer put **characters** on the screen. A character is a letter, digit, punctuation mark, or symbol used in writing. Most of the keys on your keyboard match a character. The characters you use to write C code are:

```
{ } [ ] ( ) < > = ^        0123456789
! ? . , : ; ' " _          ABCDEFGHIJKLMNOPQRSTUVWXYZ
# % & * \ | / - + ~        abcdefghijklmnopqrstuvwxyz
```

as well as space and end-of-line. Pressing Enter or Return usually makes end-of-line.

Exercise:

0. Try Program Hello Nurse. Hint: start with a copy of Program Diddly Squat.
1. Change Program Hello Nurse so that it prints your name. Hint: type something different between the double quotes ("").
2. Add \n ☞ "**backslash** en," between `Hello` and your name. The backslash character (\) is used only inside double-quotes or **single-quotes** (' ') when naming special characters like **new-line**, '\n'. You will see what new-line does when you do this exercise.
3. Remove both double-quotes, then try to compile the code. What happens? Your compiler should give you an error similar to

`Hello undeclared.`

because it thinks that `Hello` is a name, not some characters to show on the screen. Hopefully, your compiler will tell you where the error is. It *may* tell you the line number and even the column number. Look carefully at that part of your program, and make sure you understand what you are writing. *Sometimes* it is helpful to type some words of the error into a search engine—and sometimes it is *not* helpful!

printf

CHAPTER 1

Yes, We Scan

Next, you will tell the computer to read characters. Look at Program Scanner.

```
              /* Program Scanner */

     #include <stdio.h>
     int main(void) {
       printf("Hello. I am Hal. What is your name?\n");
A:;    char name[132];
B:     scanf("%s", name);
C:     printf("Hello, %s!", name);
       return 0;
     }
              /* End Program Scanner */
```

You have seen some of this before. Three lines have new stuff. The new parts are labeled A, B, and C.

You have seen something like line A before. You saw how to tell the computer to remember where anything was:

```
              void * anywhere;
```

And you saw how to tell the computer to remember a type of number called an `int`:

```
int an_integer = 0;
```

Line A tells the computer to remember an **array** ℘ "a ray," of characters:

```
char name[132];
```

The keyword char ℘ "care" or "char" is a nick-name for "character." The **square brackets**, [] mean "array." An array is two or more of the same type of thing. Each item, or **element**, in an array is a next-door neighbor of another item in the array.

In each of the last three statements, the computer is told to make an **object**. An object is a piece of information or a set of related pieces of information that are kept together. Each object has a type, a name, a value, a size, and an address.

An object's type is the kind of thing it is, such as int. A playing card's type could be ♠, ♦, ♥, or ♣. Line A **declares** ℘ "Dee Claire's" a character array object; its type is char []. To declare means to tell the computer that an object exists, and to tell its type.

An object is called by its name. Cards have names like "Jack of Spades" and "Queen of Hearts." Line A declares an object called name.

An object's size is how much space it takes up inside the computer. A card's size might be measured in units of length. An object's size is measured in characters. One character is the smallest possible size. The size of an object is different from the number of characters it takes to show its value on the screen. For example, an int might have a size of 4, even though its value might be 1. Line A declares the size of name to be 132 characters.

An object holds a value. In many card games, the ace holds the value 1, and the queen of hearts holds a value of 10. Changing the int's value does not change its size. An int with the value 42 has the same size as an int with the value 153. Two playing cards of the same size may have different values.

Line A does not tell the value of name; in a card game, you usually do not know the values of the cards in the other players' hands. Objects that are not given values contain **garbage**, which is any value at all, and no value in particular. For example, before you tell what values belong in name, those values *might* be another part of Carroll's poem:

Beware the Jabberwock, my son!/The jaws that bite, the claws that catch!/Beware the Jubjub bird, and shun/The frumious Bandersnatch!

The object name gets its value in line B:

```
scanf("%s", name);
```

The function scanf ⑨ "scan eff" is basically the opposite of printf. Instead of taking characters from your computer and putting them on the screen, it scans characters from the keyboard and puts them in the computer.

The scanf function is usually used with two or more inputs. In this case, the first input is the character array, "%s". This tells scanf what and how to scan. The pattern %s basically means, "get one word." Why isn't it %w instead of %s then? The s stands for **string**.

A string is one or more characters in a row. It could be a word, like Hello. It could also be something that *looks* like a number, such as

2.71828182845904590

A string may contain any character that your computer can see, even if that character is not one of the characters used to write in C.

The second input of scanf tells *where* to put the stuff that scanf scans. The scanf function needs an *address* for each item scanned. In C, the name of an array object is a nick-name for its address. So, the word that scanf gets in line B will be placed *where* name *points*.

Line C uses printf:

```
printf("Hello, %s!", name);
```

This printf statement is different from the one you saw in Program Hello Nurse. It has two inputs, and the first input has a %s pattern. The %s in scanf tells the computer to *scan* a character array, char [], from the keyboard. The %s in printf tells the computer to *print* a character array on the screen. Like scanf, printf needs to know the address of the string to be printed.

29

The scanf function can do more than get words. You will find other ways to use scanf in the rest of this book.

Exercise:

0. Try Program Scanner.
1. Try Program Scanner again. This time, enter a name that has a space in it, such as Hello Kitty.
2. Add /* just before the **pound sign** (#) and */ just after the greater than sign (>). Changing a statement into a comment by placing /* */ around it is called "commenting out" the statement. What happens when you try to compile the program? Compare this to what happened in № 3 of the last exercise.
3. Replace [132] with [2] so that name holds only two characters. What happens when you run the program? Try entering names of different lengths (without spaces), including some really long names, like JohnJacobJingleheimerSchmidt. When you try to cram something bigger than an object's size into that object, you can expect the program to **crash** or **blow up**, meaning to stop working. If you are running this program on a newer computer, it may not crash until you enter a name longer than about 8 or 16 characters.

Object Lessons:

You might read or hear the word "object" outside this book, and it might mean something different from what it means in C.

There is at least one more thing you should know about strings. The computer often needs to know where the end of a string is. It does this by looking for something that is not a character. This something is called a **null character**. The null character is yet another thing that stands for nothing, like void. Many functions, such as scanf, place a null character at the end of a string. When you write programs that use strings, you should make space for the null character. In Program Scanner, name points to a string with 132 characters. The longest name scanf can fit into it is 131 characters long, because the last element of name needs to be the null character.

"*I am an int. My name is Ed. I am holding the value 1 now. But, I can hold values as great as that block over yonder. My size is 4, and my address is 43.*"

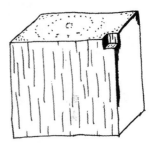

scanf, char []

PART 3

Branching Out

Now that you know about `printf` and `scanf`, you are ready to learn more keywords. You have already written your first program. And you have done so using only three keywords. With more keywords, you can write programs that do more.

You have seen some examples of telling the computer *what* to do. In this part of the book, you will learn how to tell your computer *when* to do something.

/* notes */

CHAPTER 0

♪ if **You Like to Waltz with Potatoes** ♪

—Kurt Heinecke, *The Veggie Tales Theme*

You can tell your computer *when* to do something by making it skip one or more statements. So far, your computer has been doing each part of your programs from top to bottom, but that is about to change.

Testing 1, 2, 3:

Testing is the key to making your computer skip statements. In school, the teacher makes the test, and you have to do the test. But in your programs, *you* get to make the test, and your computer has to do it.

Your computer can do only certain kinds of tests. When your teacher makes a test for you to take in school, the test is written in the same language that you speak in the class room. If your class speaks English, it would not make sense for the test to be in Klingon, Esperanto, or Church Slavonic. Since you are writing your programs in C, your tests need to be written in C.

Many tests compare two numbers. For example, "six times seven is forty-two?" (6 * 7 == 42) or "zero is less than Jake?" (0 < Jake). Your computer will take a test and return either true or false.

Zero counts as false. Any other number counts as true. So, the test (0) returns zero, which counts as false. And (Jake - 1) returns zero if Jake is equal to one, and something other than zero (true) if Jake is not equal to one. You will see more example tests in the rest of this book.

Any **expression** 🦻 "ex press shun" can be a test. An expression is something that returns a value. An expression could be something as simple as a single number.

Small Potatoes:

Look at Program Small Potatoes. Line A declares an `int` named `item_number`. Line B gets a value for `item_number` from the keyboard. I will explain the details later. Let's get to the heart of the matter: the `if` statement. Line C has an `if` statement. An `if` statement has three parts:

0. the `if` keyword,
1. a test, and
2. a statement.

The test is an expression inside parentheses (). It comes right after the `if` keyword.

What does your computer do with an `if` statement? First, it does the test. If result of the test is false, the computer skips the statement that comes right after the parentheses (). If the result of the test is true, the computer does what the statement says to do.

In Line C, the computer finds out if you entered 1. If you did, the computer prints a sad message. If you did not enter a 1, the statement with the sad message is skipped.

Taking Your Order:

I said I would tell you more about the `scanf` statement found on line B. You saw what the `%s` pattern does in the "Yes, We Scan" chapter. Whereas the `%s` pattern tells `scanf` to "get one string," The `%i` pattern tells `scanf` to "get one `int`." You need to tell `scanf` *where* to put the `int`. This happens in the second input of `scanf`. Putting only `item_number` for the second input of `scanf` does not make sense, because `item_number` is a nickname for the *value* of `item_number`. But, if you put an ampersand (&) in front of an object's name, the computer will return that object's address, and that is what we want. So, in line

B, scanf takes the characters you enter, makes an int from them, and copies the value to where item_number holds its value.

Exercise:

0. Try Program Small Potatoes. Enter a 1.
1. Try Program Small Potatoes again. Enter a 0.
2. Try Program Small Potatoes yet again. Enter a 1, followed by some gobbledygook, such as amanaplanacanalpanama. The computer does not care what comes after the 1, because you did not tell it to do anything with those characters.

```
            /* Program Small Potatoes */

#include <stdio.h>

  int main(void) {
    printf(
      "Welcome to McDenwood's."
      "We sell fries, and that's all."
      "May I take your order?\n"
      " 0. Nothing\n"
      " 1. Fries\n"
    );
A:; int item_number;
B:  scanf("%i", & item_number);
C:  if (item_number == 1)
      printf("Sorry, we are out of fries!");

    return 0;
  }
          /* End Program Small Potatoes */
```

if

CHAPTER 1

if You'd Rather not Waltz with Potatoes

"Is there anything else?"
"Yes, exactly!"
"Exactly what?"
"else!"
"Else what?"
"That's what—else!"

In the last chapter, you learned about the `if` statement. You learned how to make the computer do something only if some other thing is *true*. You can also tell the computer to do something else if that other thing is *false*.

Program More Potatoes has an example. Program More Potatoes is the same as Program Small Potatoes, except for line D. (If you type in Program More Potatoes, start with a copy of Program Small Potatoes.)

Line D tells the computer what to do when you type something other than 1. Your computer looks for an `else` keyword after each `if` statement. It will do the statement after `else` only if the test you gave it in the `if` statement returned zero (false).

Exercise:

0. Try Program More Potatoes. Enter 0.
1. Try Program More Potatoes. Enter 1.
2. Make the computer print something that makes more sense if you enter something other than 1.

else

```
            /* Program More Potatoes */

    #include <stdio.h>

    int main(void) {
      printf(
        "Welcome to McDenwood's."
        "We sell fries, and that's all."
        "May I take your order?\n"
        " 0. Nothing\n"
        " 1. Fries\n"
      );
      int item_number;
      scanf("%i", & item_number);
      if (item_number == 1)
        printf("Sorry, we are all out of fries!");
/*D*/ else
        printf("Would you like fries with that?");
      return 0;
    }
            /* End Program More Potatoes */
```

Another Statement:

You can have more than one statement inside your if and else
statements. To do this, you use braces, for example:

```
if (item_number == 1) {
   printf("Sorry, we are all out of fries!\n");
   printf("Bye!");
}
else {
   printf("Would you like fries with that?\n");
   printf("Nevermind, we're out of fries!");
}
```

CHAPTER 2

After `while`, Crocodile

I like fries. So we are going to continue adding to our example from the last chapter. Program Curly Fries adds a **loop** to Program More Potatoes so that the weird guy who takes your order keeps asking until you order fries.

A loop is part of a program that runs more than once. There are several kinds of loops. Program Curly Fries uses a `while` loop. In a `while` loop, your computer does a test. If the test result is not zero (true), the computer does the stuff inside the `while` loop. Here's the idea:

```
while ( this_is_true ) do_this();
```

or

```
while ( this_is_true ) { do_this(); and_this(); }
```

The first form (without braces) is used when only one statement is in the loop. The second form is used when more than one statement is in the loop. The form of the `while` statement is the same as the form of the `if` statement. The only difference is the keyword at the beginning.

The first place that Program Curly Fries is really different from Program More Potatoes is on Line A. Here, `item_number` gets the value 0. You need to tell the computer what value to give `item_number` because that value is tested in line B. If you don't give `item_number` a value, its value *could* be 1, and that would mess us up.

In line B, the test compares the value of `item_number` with 1. The code in parentheses (`item_number != 1`), tests whether `item_number` is *not* equal to 1. In C, the exclamation point means "not," so `!=` means "not equal to."

Line B is the beginning of a `while` loop. If the expression inside the parentheses `()` is true, the computer will do the stuff inside the braces `{}`. Those braces open at the end of line B and close just before the `Crocodile` label. A label is a name followed by a colon.

Notice how the closing brace lines up with the beginning of the `while` keyword. Placing the closing brace there makes it easier to see what it belongs to. It belongs to the `while` loop.

A `while` statement is the same as an `if` statement, except that when the computer gets to the end of the `while` loop, it goes back to the beginning, does the test again, and, if the test is true, it does the loop again.

Exercise:

0. Try Program Curly Fries. The program will keep asking to take your order until you enter 1.
1. Change line A so that the value of `item_number` starts out as 1. Then, compile an run the program again.

Exclamation Proclamation:

In C, the exclamation point means "not." So, `!=` means "not equal to," `!0` means "not zero" or "not false," and `!any_expression` means (`any_expression == 0`). By the way, the `==` symbol means equals, as in, "does zero equal zero?" Remember, if you are *telling* the computer what something *should* be equal to, use the equals sign (=) and if you are *asking* the computer whether two things are equal, use double equals (==).

```
              /* Program Curly Fries */

       #include <stdio.h>

       int main(void) {
         printf("Welcome to McDenwood's. We sell fries,"
                "and that's all.");
/*A*/    int item_number = 0;
/*B*/    while (item_number != 1) {
             printf("May I take your order?\n"
                 " 0. Nothing\n"
                 " 1. Fries\n"
                 " 2. Something else\n");
             scanf("%i", & item_number);
             if (item_number == 1)
               printf("Sorry, we are all out of fries!\n");
             else
/*C*/          printf("All we sell is fries.\n");
         }
Crocodile:
       return 0;
       }

              /* End Program Curly Fries */
```

while

CHAPTER 3

See You Later, Alligator

It is silly to try to figure out whether you want fries before you are asked, but that is what Line B of Program Curly Fries is doing the first time the computer gets there. It would make more sense if you could see the menu first, then decide what you want. C has a way for you to do this. It's called a do loop.

A do loop begins with the keyword do and *ends* with a while statement. In between do and while, there are one or more statements in braces {}. Program Fry Menu has an example. There, the while statement from Program Curly Fries is moved to the end of the braces, and the keyword do is placed before the braces, just after the Alligator label.

Program Fry Menu gets a value for item_number from the keyboard. Only then does the computer test item_number. So, Program Fry Menu does not need to give item_number a starting value as in Program Curly Fries.

Exercise:

Try Program Fry Menu. The program will keep asking to take your order until you enter 1. Notice that Program Fry Menu does exactly the same thing as Program Curly Fries. There are many ways to do the same thing in C.

```
                  /* Program Fry Menu */

    #include <stdio.h>

    int main(void) {
      printf("Welcome to McDenwood's. We sell fries,"
          "and that's all.");
      int item_number;
Alligator:
      do {
        printf("May I take your order?\n"
            " 1. Fries\n"
            " 2. Something else\n");
        scanf("%i", & item_number);
        if (item_number == 1)
          printf("Sorry, we are all out of fries!\n");
        else
          printf("All we sell is fries.\n");
      } while (item_number != 1);
      return 0;
    }
                  /* End Program Fry Menu */
```

Leaping before You Look:

Someone older and wiser than yourself may have told you "look before you leap." But it's okay to leap before you look—*if* you already *know* what you might have found out by looking. In Program Fry Menu, you *know* you will show the menu at least once, so you do it without looking at item_number.

CHAPTER 4

Just in case

You have been using `if` statements to decide what to print on the screen. These `if` statements are nice when you want to choose between two things. If you want to choose among more than two things, the `switch` statement may be better. The `switch` statement tells the computer what to do for different `case`'s. Let's look at an example: Program Case of Fries.

On line A of Program Case of Fries, the computer looks at `item_number`.

The computer then goes from `case` to `case`, looking for something that matches `item_number`. If it finds a match, it does the statements that come after the matching item. The `default` keyword will match anything. You do not have to put `default` in your case statement, but you may.

The computer will keep going through all the cases until it is told to **jump** out of the `switch` statement. Jumping is when the computer skips statements. The computer can jump forward or backward. One way to get the computer to jump out is to use the `break` statement. When the computer sees `break`, it will jump to the statement just after the closing brace of the switch statement (line B).

Enough reading! You should try Program Case of Fries in order to understand `switch`, `case`, `default`, and `break`.

Exercise:

0. Try Program Case of Fries. Enter the digit 1. The computer will ask you if you would like a drink. It keeps going on to case 2, asking if you would like fries with that. It keeps going to case 3, where it sees the break statement. Then it jumps out of the switch statement and finds return 0, which ends the program.

1. Try Program Case of Fries again. This time enter the digit 2. The computer skips over case 1, because it does not match the 2 you entered. It would not make sense to ask if you would like a drink— obviously, you do, because you just ordered one! The computer keeps going to case 3, and so on, as when you entered a 1.

2. Try Program Case of Fries *again*. This time, enter the digit 3. The computer skips case 1 and case 2 because they do not match the digit you entered. Then, the computer finds a match at case 3 and break's out of the switch statement.

3. Try Program Case of Fries yet again. This time, enter something other than 1, 2, or 3. The only thing that matches your input is default, because default matches anything. The computer tells you "we're all out of that." You asked for something that is not on the menu.

4. Change the program so that, when you ask for fries, the computer asks if you want a drink.

5. Change the program by adding another menu item and another case.

/* Program Case of Fries */

```c
#include <stdio.h>
int main(void) {
  int item_number;

  printf(
    "Welcome to McDenwood's."
    "May I take your order?\n"
    " 1. Sandwich\n"
    " 2. Drink\n"
    " 3. Fries\n"
  );

  scanf("%i", & item_number);

A:   switch (item_number) {
    case 1:
      printf("Would you like a drink?\n");
    case 2:
      printf("Would you like fries with that?");
    case 3: break;
    default: printf("We're all out of that.\n");
  }

B:   return 0;
  }
```
        /* End Program Case of Fries */

Limited Case:

When you write switch statements, the parentheses after the switch keyword must be the name of an integer or character object. So, you cannot ask the computer to look through case's of strings, character arrays, or pointers.

switch, case, default, break

CHAPTER 5

Where did you go? Out. What did you do? Nothing.

—Smith and Spanfeller

If you want the computer to skip part of your program, you can use goto 𝔇 "go to." A goto statement has two parts: the keyword goto and a label name. When the computer sees goto and a label name, the computer goes *directly* to the statement labeled with that name. (It does not pass "GO," and it does not collect $200.) Remember: a label is a name followed by a colon. Labels must be put at the beginning of statements.

The goto statement is **controversial** "con trow verse shall." Some people like goto and others don't.

SHHH! HERE'S A DIRTY LITTLE SECRET: If your C code has a loop or an if statement, your compiler will write machine code that has has goto! DON'T TELL ANYONE! SHHH!

Exercise:

0. Try Program Skip the Fries.
1. Pretend there is a problem with the scanf statement in Program Case of Fries. Make the rest of the program work by giving a value to item_number using a statement like item_number = 1; and using goto to skip over the scanf statement.

```
                /* Program Skip The Fries */

     #include <stdio.h>
     int main(void) {
       int item_number;
       printf(
         "Welcome to McDenwood's."
         "May I take your order?\n"
         " 1. Sandwich\n"
         " 2. Drink\n"
         " 3. Fries\n"
       );
A:     goto B;
       scanf("%i", & item_number);
       switch (item_number) {
         case 1:
           printf("Would you like a drink?\n");
         case 2:
           printf("Would you like fries with that?");
         case 3:
           break;
         default:
           printf("We're all out of that.\n");
       }
B:     return 0;
     }
              /* End Program Skip The Fries */
```

CHAPTER 6

for

In the After While, Crocodile chapter, you learned about while loops. In the See You Later, Alligator chapter, you learned about do loops. There is one more kind of loop in C. This third kind of loop is called a for loop. Just as a while loop begins with the while keyword, and a do loop begins with the do keyword, a for loop begins with the for keyword. The while loop and the for loop are closely related. Look for some ways they are the same in this example:

```
        for (
/*A*/     j = 0;
/*B*/     j < 9;
/*C*/     j = j + 1;
        )
        {
/*D*/     printf("%i", j);
        }
```

Using the letters shown, a for loop follows the pattern A-BDC-BDC-BDC . . . In the loop, the computer sets the value of j to zero once only (line A). Each time the computer begins the loop, it does the test j < 9 (line B). If j *is* less than 9, the computer shows the value of j on the screen (line D). The %i pattern tells printf to show an int. Next, the computer adds one to the value of j (line C). Then, the computer checks whether j < 9, and so on.

Many programmers use for loops that look like this:

for

```
      /* This loop repeats this_many times. */
      for ( j = 0; j < this_many; j++ ) {
          do_something();
          do_something_else();
      }
```

or this:

```
      for ( j = 0; j < this_many; j++ ) statement;
```

The expression j++ ⑨ "jay plus plus" is short for j = j + 1.

Exercise:

0. Try Program Count.
1. Change Program Count by adding the digit 3 between % and i, then try it again. You should see a change in how the numbers print. The digit 3 tells printf to use at least three spaces to show an int.
2. Repeat № 1, but put 12 (instead of 3) between % and i.
3. Change Program Count by replacing ++ with += 1. Then try Program Count again. Does the output change? The symbol += ⑨ "plus equals" tells the computer to add the value on the right side of the += symbol to the object whose name is on the left side of the += symbol.
4. Change Program Count by replacing += 1 with += 2. Try Program Count again. You should see the computer count by twos.
5. Change Program Count to make the computer stop at a different number. Hint: how does the for loop in Program Count know when to stop?
6. Change Program Count to make the computer count by 5's.
7. Change Program Count to make the computer count by 10's.
8. Change Program Count by replacing j < 9 with j < 0.
9. Try Program Chart. Program Chart has a **nested loop**, a loop inside a loop.

```
               /* Program Count */

#include <stdio.h>

int main(void) {
    int i;
    for ( i = 0; i < 9; i++ ) printf("%i ", i);
    return 0;
}

             /* End Program Count */




               /* Program Chart */

#include <stdio.h>
int main(void) {
    int i, j;

    for (i = 0; i < 10; i++) {

      for (j = 0; j < 10; j++) printf("%3i", i + j);
      printf("\n");

    }

    return 0;
}

             /* End Program Chart */
```

for

CHAPTER 7

To Be continue'd

Normally, the computer goes all the way around a loop before going back to the beginning. But you can change this. You can tell the computer to jump *from* somewhere inside the loop *to* the beginning of the loop. You can do this with a `continue` statement.

Program Chart Two contains a `continue` statement on line A. The `continue` statement is part of an `if` statement. The test of the `if` statement has a percent sign. You have seen the percent sign before, but only as part of the first input of a `printf` or `scanf` statement. When you use the percent sign between two numbers, the result is the remainder of a division problem. For example, 21 ÷ 10 is 2, remainder 1; so 21 % 10 returns 1.

Exercise:

0. Try Program Chart Two. The hundreds chart should appear on the screen. The computer starts a new line after each multiple of ten.
1. Change Program Chart Two by putting the ++ symbol after i. In other words, change ++i to i++. Then, try the program again. The statement ++i adds 1 to i, then returns i. The statement i++ returns i, then adds 1 to i.
2. Change Program Chart Two by replacing 100 with 200. Then, try the program again.
3. Change Program Chart Two by replacing % 10 with % 20. Then, try the program again.

```
              /* Program Chart Two */

  #include <stdio.h>

    int main(void) {
      int i;
      for (i = 0; i < 100; i++) {
        printf("%5i", ++i);
A:      if (i % 10) continue;
        printf("\n");
    }
    return 0;
  }
              /* End Program Chart Two */
```

PART 4

Assorted Objects

You have already learned about the `int`, `char`, and `char []` (character array) types. In this part, you will learn about other types. You will also learn how to make your own types.

/* notes */

CHAPTER 0

Halflings

So far, you have used `int`'s to hold integers from -32,767 to +32,767. In C, there are also two other kinds of numbers: **floating point** and `enum` 𝄞 "ee numb." You will learn more about floating point and `enum` types in this chapter.

Floating Point:

Floating point numbers can hold integers below -32,767 and beyond 32,767. One such number is 301,107,070,500,000,000,000,000. Floating point numbers can also hold proper fractions, such as ½, and improper fractions, such as ⅗.

Floating point numbers have three parts. The first two parts are the same as the two parts of an `int`: a sign and a sequence of digits. The sign tells whether the number is positive or negative. Usually, you do not write the sign of a positive number (+), but you may. The second part is a sequence of digits.

The third part of a floating point number is an **exponent** 𝄞 "ex Poe nent." The exponent tells where to put the decimal point. The exponent works like the trick for multiplying or dividing by ten. The decimal point starts out at one place, then moves to the right or left.

The big number in the first paragraph of this chapter can be broken down into the three parts of a floating point number: a positive sign, the sequence of digits 3011070705, and an exponent of 14, meaning to move the decimal point 14 places to the right. Your computer probably does not keep track of floating point numbers *exactly* this way. And

C does *not* have a rule that tells *exactly* how to keep track of floating point numbers. However, this is the basic idea.

You might think that there is a limit to how many digits a floating point number can hold. You would be right. Those limits depend on your system. *For this reason, you should* not *assume that a floating point number is* exactly *equal to any particular number.* For example, if you ask the computer to hold the value ⅓, it *might* see 0.333333. Now, 0.333333 is *close* to ⅓, but it is *not exactly* ⅓.

There are three types of floating point numbers in C: `float`, `double`, and `long double`. You will see how to use them in this chapter.

The keyword `double` is a funny name for a floating point number. It is called this because a `double` usually takes up twice as much space as a `float`. A `long double` may use more space than a `double`. But on many systems, `long double` is the same as `double`! A double can hold numbers up to . . .

1,000,000,000,000,000,000,000,000,000,000,000,000,000,
000,000,000,000,000,000,000,000,000,000,000,000,000,000,
000,000,000,000,000,000,000,000,000,000,000,000,000,000,
000,000,000,000,000,000,000,000,000,000,000,000,000,000,
000,000,000,000,000,000,000,000,000,000,000,000,000,000,
000,000,000,000,000,000,000,000,000,000,000,000,000,000,
000,000,000,000,000,000,000,000,000,000,000,000,000,000,
000,000,000,000,000,000,000,000,000,000,000,000,000,000,
000,000,000,000,000,000,000,000,000,000,000,000,000,000,
000,000,000,000,000,000,000,000,000,000,000,000,000,000,
000,000,000,000,000,000,000,000,000,000,000,000,000,000,
000,000,000,000,000,000,000,000,000,000,000,000,000,000,
000,000,000,000,000,000,000,000,000,000,000,000,000,000,
000,000,000,000,000,000,000,000,000,000,000,000,000,000,
000,000,000,000,000,000,000,000,000,000,000,000,000,000,
000,000,000,000,000,000,000,000,000,000,000,000,000,000,
000,000,000,000,000,000,000,000,000,000,000,000,000,000,

000 or so.

"If you can read this, you don't need glasses!"
—Brooks, Meehan, and Graham, *Spaceballs*

enum:

The enum type gets its name from "**enumerated**" 𝔇 "ee new myrrh ray Ted." The enum's are groups of special names that you make. Each name is a nickname for an integer.

You get to decide whether the integer that goes with a name is important. In one program, you might decide that penny, nickel, dime, and quarter should be nicknames for 1, 5, 10, and 25. But in another program, you might decide that those same names should go with 0, 1, 2, and 3. You can even decide that you don't care which integers go with which names, but that each name should go with a different number. You might want some names to keep track of what kind of metal a coin is made of: gold, silver, copper, and Nickel, for example. Remember: C is case sensitive, so nickel and Nickel are not the same thing. It is probably not important which integers go with which metal, but it is important that the integer that goes with gold is *different* from the one that goes with silver, and so on.

Halfling Price:

Program Halflings shows the prices for hobbit Lego® minifigures.

The first thing on Line A is the phrase enum hobbitses. This says that a group of names called hobbitses is about to be enumerated. The next thing on line A is a set of braces. Inside those braces is a list of names. Each of these names is a nickname for a value. Program Halflings does not tell what those values are, but their values are **implied** 𝔇 "imp lied." Something implied is unsaid or unwritten, but is present. The compiler will match the names with the values 0, 1, 2, and 3. If there were a fifth item, its value would be 4, and so on. After the names have been defined, they can be used as if they were int's.

In Program Scanner, you declared a character array:

```
char name[132];
```

In Program Halflings, line B, defines an array of double's. There is no number between the brackets [], because that number is *implied*.

There's that word again! The array is defined to contain the values 4.17, 6.00, 5.78, and 4.58.

In line C, Program Halflings does something really cool. It declares an object called hobbit (not a dirty, nasty hobbit). And that object has a type that *you* made in line A; hobbit has the type enum hobbitses. The hobbit object can hold frodo, merry, pippin, or sam.

Line D has a for loop. The loop goes through each value of hobbit. Inside the loop, the printf statement shows a price that matches the hobbit. That is what price[hobbit] means. For example, when hobbit == merry, the value 6.00 is shown. The merry[th] value of price is 6.00.

Line D also has a % pattern in the printf statement. The space between the percent sign and the decimal point tells the computer to put a space in front if each number. The decimal point and the 2 tell printf to show two digits after the decimal point.

Exercise:

0. Try Program Halflings.
1. Add one more name to the enum statement (suggestion: bilbo) and one more price to the price array. Change the condition (i <= sam) inside the for loop so that the price of the new hobbit will be shown. Try Program Halflings again.
2. Change double to float. Try Program Halflings again.

Doubling Up on Floating Point Patterns:

The printf statement will make a double from the float, and then show the double. That is why you can use a %f pattern with both float and double. If you want to use printf with a long double, use %Lf, not %f.

```
              /* Program Halflings */

     #include <stdio.h>

     int main(void) {

A:;   enum hobbitses { frodo, merry, pippin, sam };
B:;   double price[] = { 4.17, 6.00, 5.78, 4.58 };

C:;   enum hobbitses hobbit;
D:    for (hobbit = frodo; hobbit <= sam; hobbit++)
      printf("% .2f", price[hobbit]);

      return 0;
     }
              /* End Program Halflings */
```

double, enum, float

CHAPTER 1

To 2^{16} . . . and Beyond!

You have learned that the numbers in your computer are either integers or floating point numbers. You learned about the three types of floating point numbers: `float`, `double`, and `long double`. There are nine kinds of integers in C. Together, these are called the **integral** 🦻 "int egg roll" types.

Each type of integer has a different range. A range goes from a **minimum** 🦻 "mini mum" value to a **maximum** 🦻 "max i mum" value. The minimum is the smallest or least. The maximum is the biggest or greatest. *Max.* stands for maximum and *min.* stands for minimum.

You have already learned that the range of an `int` depends on your system. However, you can be sure that an `int` can hold values as high as 32,767 and as low as -32,767. The other types of integers also have ranges that depend on your system. C does not define the range of values for any type. However, C does define special names that you can use to find out the range of each type.

The nine integral types are shown in Table 0. Each row of Table 0 tells about one type. The keywords you use to make an object of that type are in the first column. The second and third columns have nicknames for the minimum and maximum values that an object of that type can hold. (You can use these nicknames as if they were numbers.) The "Minimum Range" column has two values. If a number is between the two values, you can be sure that an object of the type listed can hold that number. And this will be true for *any* system.

`long, short, signed, unsigned`

Exercise:

Use #include <limits.h> and write a program that displays the integer type names along with their limits. Hints: Use the printf statement. Use %i in the first input of printf to display CHAR_MAX, SCHAR_MAX, and INT_MAX. Use %u in the first input to display UCHAR_MAX and UINT_MAX; %hi for SHRT_MAX; %hu for USHRT_MAX; %li for LONG_MAX; and %lu for ULONG_MAX. BIG HINT: look at the program at the end of this chapter!

Table 0: The Integral Types

Type	Min. Value	Max. Value	Minimum Range		Size	Pattern†
char	CHAR_MIN	CHAR_MAX	0 to	127	1	%c
signed char	SCHAR_MIN	SCHAR_MAX	-127 to	127	1	%c
unsigned char	0	UCHAR_MAX	0 to	255	1	%c
short	SHRT_MIN	SHRT_MAX	-32,767 to	32,767	*	%hi
unsigned short	0	SHRT_MAX	0 to	65,535	*	%hu
int	INT_MIN	INT_MAX	-32,767 to	32,767	*	%i
unsigned int	0	UINT_MAX	0 to	65,535	*	%u
long	LONG_MIN	LONG_MAX	-2,147,483,647 to	2,147,483,647	*	%li
unsigned long	0	ULONG_MAX	0 to	4,294,967,295	*	%lu

* Character types have size 1. The size of other types depends on your system.

† Use this pattern with printf. The %i pattern can be used to show the number of a character.

```c
#include <stdio.h>
#include <limits.h>
int main(void) {
    printf("Type          %12s%12s\n",      "Minimum",   "Maximum");
    printf("------------------------------------------\n");
    printf("unsigned char%12i"   "%12i\n",   0,          UCHAR_MAX);
    printf(" signed char%12i"    "%12i\n",   SCHAR_MIN,  SCHAR_MAX);
    printf("       char%12i"     "%12i\n",   CHAR_MIN,   CHAR_MAX);
    printf("unsigned short%12hu" "%12hu\n",  0,          USHRT_MAX);
    printf("      short%12hi"    "%12hi\n",  SHRT_MIN,   SHRT_MAX);
    printf("unsigned      %12u"  "%12u\n",   0,          UINT_MAX);
    printf("        int%12i"     "%12i\n",   INT_MIN,    INT_MAX);
    printf("unsigned long%12lu"  "%12lu\n",  0,          ULONG_MAX);
    printf("       long%12li"    "%12li\n",  LONG_MIN,   LONG_MAX);
    printf("------------------------------------------\n");
    return 0;
}
```

CHAPTER 2

Building Structures

Let's pretend you are going to use your computer to keep track of your Pokemon cards. You could keep track of a Pokemon's HP using an unsigned type. You could keep track of a Pokemon's name using a char [] (character array). And, you could keep track of a Pokemon's type with your own enum type that you define like this:

```
enum Type { fire, iron, dragon, fairy };
```

If you know about more Pokemon types, you can include them in the list.

You already know about unsigned, char [], and enum objects. Each of these types of objects can hold *one* trait, or **member**, of a Pokemon. But a Pokemon has *many* traits. It would be nice if there were an object that could keep track of all of the traits of a Pokemon. C does not have a pokemon type, but C does allow you to *make* a pokemon type.

A Pokemon of Your Own:

You can make a pokemon type by putting objects together in a **structure** 𝔇 "struck sure." So, you can make a structure called pokemon that has HP, a name, and a type. You tell the computer that you want to define a structure by using the keyword struct 𝔇 "strucked," like this:

```
struct pokemon {
  char[40] name;
  unsigned hp;
  enum Type type;
};
```

This just tells the names and types of the traits of a pokemon. To tell your computer to keep track of a *certain* pokemon, you need to declare one, like this:

```
struct pokemon myPokemon;
```

This is like the way enum's work: first you define what a new type of object can hold, then you make an object of that type.

Here, Skitty, Skitty:

My son Edward has a "Skitty" Pokemon card. To tell your computer to keep track of this card, you could define it like this:

```
struct pokemon skitty = { "Skitty", 50, iron };
```

the stuff on the left side of the equals sign tells the computer to make a pokemon structure called skitty. The stuff on the right side of the equals sign tells the computer to put in "Skitty" for the name, 50 for the hp, and iron for the type. The items inside the braces {} must be in the same order as in the structure type definition.

You could also define the members of skitty like this:

```
skitty.hp = 50;
skitty.type = iron;
```

The dot operator (.) is placed between a structure name and a member name. So, skitty.hp means the member of skitty called hp. When you give a value to a member of a pokemon, you have to tell the computer which pokemon *and* which member. That's why we have skitty.hp = 50 and not just skitty = 50 or hp = 50.

String Quirks:

You might think that you could define the `name` of `skitty` like this:

```
skitty.name = "Skitty";
```

But that is *not* allowed in C. You can't use the equals sign to tell the computer what a `char []` should hold—unless you do it as part of the declaration (as in the last section). You use a function called `strncpy`:

```
#include <string.h>
strncpy(skitty.name, "Skitty", 39);
```

This copies "Skitty" to the first 6 elements of `skitty.name`, and fills the other elements of `skitty.name` with the null character. (You learned about the null character in the "Yes, We Scan" chapter.) To be **safe**, you should put a null character at the end of `skitty.name`, like this:

```
skitty.name[39] = '\0';
```

Being "safe" means to do things in ways that avoid crashes. Now, `skitty.name` is a character array, `char []`. But the 39th item in that array is just a *single* character, `char`. When you put *single* quotes around something, you are telling the computer about a *single* character. The pattern \0 within single quotes means the null character. You can also use \0 inside of a string or character array to mean the null character.

If the number of characters you try to put into a character array is greater than the size of that character array, or if the character array does not end in a null character, it is easy to cause a crash. C has many functions that do not stop until the null character is reached.

Exercise:

0. Try Program Pokemon. That program has two functions: `show` and `main`. The `main` function uses `show` to display the traits of each Pokemon. Since `show` is used before it is defined, the program

struct

needs to have a function **prototype** 🄿 "pro toe type." Function prototypes are similar to object declarations: they tell the computer that a function exists, what the return type is, and what the inputs are. The function prototype for show is found just before main.

1. Change Program Pokemon so that more Pokemon types are allowed. Add names to the list.

/* Program Pokemon */

```
#include <string.h>
#include <stdio.h>

enum Type { iron, fire };

struct pokemon {
    char name[40];
    enum Type type;
    unsigned hp;
};

void show(struct pokemon p);

int main(void) {

    struct pokemon skitty = { "Skitty", iron, 50 };

    struct pokemon unnamed;
    strncpy(unnamed.name, "", 39);
    unnamed.name[39] = '\0';
    unnamed.hp = 40;
    unnamed.type = fire;

    show(skitty);
    show(unnamed);

    return 0;
}
```

```
void show(struct pokemon p) {
    printf("name: %s\n", p.name);
    printf("HP: %u\n", p.hp);
    printf("type: ");
    switch (p.type) {
      case iron: { printf("Iron"); break; }
      case fire: { printf("Fire"); break; }
    }
    printf("\n\n");
    return;
}
                    /* End Program Pokemon */
```

struct

CHAPTER 3

Return of the Fry Guy

Structures store each member in its own space. But, sometimes it makes sense to store members in the same space. A **union** 👂 "yoon yun" is like a structure except for this difference. When you give a value to one of the members of a union, the values of the other members are erased, because of the shared space. You tell the computer to build a union by using the keyword union.

So, I guess there are actually two differences between structures and unions: the shared space thing, and the keyword. It's that simple. But, I'll still give you an example in the Exercise.

Exercise:

0. Try Program Return of the Fry Guy.
1. Add code to the program so that it repeats the order back to the customer.

```c
          /* Program Return of the Fry Guy */

enum sizeWord { small, medium, large };

union Size {
    double volume, weight;
    enum sizeWord word;
};

struct Item {
    unsigned number;
    union Size size;
};

#include <stdio.h>
int main(void) {
    struct Item item;
    printf(
      "Welcome to McDenwood's."
      "May I take your order?\n"
      " 1. Sandwich\n"
      " 2. Drink\n"
      " 3. Fries\n"
    );

scanf("%u", & item.number);

switch (item.number) {
    case 1: {
      printf("How big? Enter the weight of the patty"
             "in pounds.\n");
      scanf("%f", & item.size.weight);
      break;
    }
```

```
   case 2: {
     printf("How much?"
             "Enter the volume in ounces.\n");
     scanf("%f", & item.size.volume);
     break;
   }

   case 3: {
     printf("What size?\n"
            "%i. small\n"
            "%i. medium\n"
            "%i. large\n",
            small, medium, large);
     scanf("%i", & item.size.word);
     break;
    }
  }
  return 0;
}
        /* End Program Return of the Fry Guy */
```

union

CHAPTER 4

Def Type

"Def" is a slang word meaning "excellent." This chapter is about a def type. Read on.

In the other chapters of this part, you saw how to make your own types using `enum`, `struct`, and `union`. You can give special names to your types by using the `typedef` ♪ "type def" keyword. You can also use the `typedef` keyword to make big changes to your programs with only small changes to your code. By using `typedef`, you can write code that uses one type, then change the type at a later time. The `typedef` keyword works like this: add the keyword to the beginning of a type definition, then give the special name you want at the end. You could do this:

```
typedef enum Type { iron, fire } TYPE;
```

Then you can use TYPE instead of `enum  Type`. You could also leave out Type—you don't need it, since you have the special name, TYPE:

```
typedef enum { iron, fire } TYPE;
```

You can also make up your own names for types that are already defined, like this:

```
typedef int number;
```

This would allow you to use `number` in place of `int`.

typedef

Def Program:

Program Def Pokemon is similar to Program Pokemon. It uses
typedef'd names in several places. Line A defines the special name
Type, so you can use Type instead of enum Type. Line B defines HP
so you can use HP as the type of hp. And line C uses typedef so that
you can use pokemon instead of struct pokemon in lines D, E, and
F.

Exercise:

0. Try Program Def Pokemon.
1. Change Program Def Pokemon so that HP is an int. Imagine that
    you had written a large program that used unsigned in a lot of
    places as the type of hp. Then you discover that hp sometimes
    needs to be less than zero. You would have a lot of changes to
    make. But if you had defined your own special name for the type
    of hp, you could change just that one line of code, and everything
    else would fall into place.

```
                /* Program Def Pokemon */

       #include <stdio.h>
/*A*/  typedef enum { iron, fire } Type;
/*B*/  typedef unsigned HP;
/*C*/  typedef struct {
           char name[40];
           Type type;
           HP hp;
       } pokemon;
/*D*/  void show(pokemon p);

       int main(void) {
/*E*/      pokemon skitty = { "Skitty", iron, 50 };
           show(skitty);
           return 0;
       }

/*F*/  void show(pokemon p) {
           printf("name: %s\n", p.name);
           printf("HP: %u\n", p.hp);
           printf("type: ");
           switch (p.type) {
            case iron: { printf("Iron"); break; }
            case fire: { printf("Fire"); break; }
           }
           printf("\n\n");
           return;
       }
                /* End Program Def Pokemon */
```

```
typedef
```

PART 5

Inside, Outside, Upside Down

—Stan and Jan Berenstain

In this part, you will learn about keywords that tell the computer *how* to use objects. But, before you do this, you need to learn about **scope** and **linkage** 👂 "link age."

Scope:

Scope has to do with what can be "seen" from different parts of the program. C has four scopes: **function** scope, **file** scope, **block** scope, and **function prototype** scope (see Figure 3).

Only labels have function scope; labels can be seen only from inside their functions. Anything found between braces has block scope—anything except a label, that is. Only inputs found in a function declaration have function prototype scope. Anything not having function, block, or function prototype scope has file scope. Program Scopes Trial has comments that explain the scope of each object.

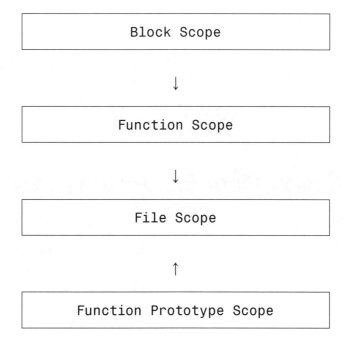

Figure 3: The Four Scopes. When your computer is in one scope of your program, it can "see" objects there. It can also see objects that can be reached by following the arrows. When your computer is in one block, it can see objects in that block, in the function where the block is located, and in file scope. When in function scope, it can see function scope and file scope. When in file scope it can see file scope only. When in function prototype scope, it can see function prototype scope and file scope.

```
                  /* Program Scopes Trial */

    int i;                  /* i has file scope. It is */
                            /* outside of any function.*/

    int function (int j); /* j has function proto-   */
                            /* type scope. It is in    */
                            /* the list of inputs in a */
                            /* function prototype.     */
    int main (void) {
        int k;              /* k has block scope. It   */
                            /* is between braces.       */

A:      k = i;              /* A has function scope.    */
                            /* It is a label.           */

        return 0;
    }

    int function (int j){ return 0; }

              /* End Program Scopes Trial */
```

Normally, when you use a name, your computer looks for that name in the current scope. If it does not find the name there, it looks outside, in the scope that contains the current scope. The search continues until the computer finds the name or until it reaches file scope and does not find the name there.

Program Daddies shows some different ways your computer will find names.

On line A, your computer looks for a character array named head to put in place of the first %s pattern. It finds head in the current scope, which is the block of code between the pair of braces that starts two lines above line A and ends on the line below line A. The definition of head includes the keyword const after the char keyword. This tells the compiler to keep you from writing code that changes the elements of the array.

Next, the program tells your computer to look for a character array named blah to put in place of the second %s pattern. It does not find it in the current scope. It then looks outside, between the braces that begin and end main. It does not find it there, so it looks outside of main, in file scope. It finds blah in file scope. (The blah character array is also defined using the keyword const.)

In line B, your computer looks for a character array named head to put in place of the first %s pattern. It does not find it in the current scope. It then looks outside, between the braces that begin and end main. It does not find it there, so it looks outside of main, in file scope. It finds head in file scope. (This head is also defined using the const keyword.)

```
                /* Program Daddies */

    #include <stdio.h>
    char const blah[] = " is the head of ";
    int main(void) {
        char const head[] = "I don't know who";
        {
          char const head[] = "James";
A:        printf("%s%sJerusalem.\n", head, blah);
        }
        {
B:        printf("%s%sthe Moon.\n", head, blah);
        }
        return 0;
    }

            /* End Program Daddies */
```

CHAPTER 0

extern **(Outside)**

In the introduction of this part, you learned how the computer *normally* looks for names. But, you can tell the computer to act in a different way. You do this by using the extern 𝔇 "ex turn" keyword. If you use the extern keyword when declaring an object, the computer will look for that name in file scope. It will "jump" over any block or function boundaries that are in between.

In line C of Program Pappas your computer looks for a character array named head to put in place of the first %s pattern. Notice that in the same block, in the line just above line C, the extern keyword is in the front of the declaration of head. This tells the computer not to act normally. Since, in line C, head is extern, your computer will search for and find head in file scope.

Exercise:

0. Try Program Pappas.
1. Change some of the values in the **assignment statements** and try the program again. Assignment statements have an equals sign (=) and tell what value an object should hold.
2. Add your own block inside main. Make it show one of the head's.

```
                /* Program Pappas */


    #include <stdio.h>
    char head[] = "Linus";
    char blah[] = " is the head of ";
    int main(void) {
      char head[] = "I don't know who";
      {
        char head[] = "James";
        printf("%s%sJerusalem.\n", head, blah);
      }
      {
        printf("%s%sthe Moon.\n", head, blah);
      }
      {
        extern char head[];
C:      printf("%s%sRome.\n", head, blah);
      }
      return 0;
    }
                /* Program Pappas */
```

CHAPTER 1

`static` **Klingons Inside!**

Normally, your computer will forget the values of objects when it goes from one block to another or from one function to another. But you can tell the computer to remember those values by using the `static` keyword. Program Shoot has a simple example that could be part of a game.

In Program Shoot, a function called `shoot` does most of the work.

Line A is inside the definition of `shoot`. If you cover up the keyword `static`, this is something you have seen before. This line tells the computer to make `arrow`; `arrow` is an `unsigned` integer. Line A also tells the computer that `arrow` should hold the value 9. The `static` keyword tells the computer to remember the value of arrow, even after it has finished `shoot`. The `static` keyword also tells your computer that the *first* time the computer gets to line A, it will give the value 9 to `arrow`. All other times your computer gets to `shoot`, it will remember the value of `arrow` from last time. If `shoot` were part of a game, you could say that the player starts with nine arrows, but the number of arrows could change each time he `shoot`'s.

Line B defines an array of character pointers. Notice the [] symbol for array, the `char` keyword for character, and the * for pointer.

The definition in line B also has the keyword `const`. The `const` keyword after * tells your compiler to make sure you do not write code that tries to change the character pointers in the array. The `const` keyword after `char` tells your compiler to make sure you do not write code that tries to change the characters being pointed to by the elements of the array.

Element zero of the array points to the character array `twang\n`, and element one of the array points to the character array `ffftp\n`. The name of the array of character pointers is `onomatopoeia` 𝄐 "on no ma toe pee yuh." Onomatopoeia are words that sound like what they mean. "Twang" is the sound of a bowstring being plucked. "Ffftp" is the sound of an arrow flying past a bow.

Line C has an `if` statement. You have seen `if` statements before. But, there is something new between the parentheses: the && symbol. The && symbol tells your computer to look to the left and right. If the value to the left is not equal to zero *and* the value to the right is not equal to zero, the expression returns !0, or "true." Otherwise, the expression returns 0, or "false."

Together, the idea of lines C and D is: if you have any arrows left and you try to shoot one, you shoot one. And, if you don't have any arrows, but try to shoot the bow, you don't shoot any arrows.

Line E has another new symbol (-=). This means "subtract the value on the right from the object on the left." Line E takes away one arrow if there are any to take away.

Line F has a `printf` statement. This one is different from the other `printf` statements you have seen. So far, you have been using the `printf` statement with a first input that is something between double quotes. But, you can also use a character pointer. The character pointer should point to a sequence of characters that `printf` understands. Since `actual_arrows` will be either zero or one, the first input of `printf` points to either `"twang!\n"` or `"ffftp!\n"`. These strings were defined in line B.

Line G has the first statement of `main`. It is a `while` loop. This while loop does nothing as long as shoot returns "true." Notice that shoot returns the number of arrows left. So, this loop will go until there are no more arrows.

Line H is exactly the same as line G, but your computer will have different output. The `while` loop of line H ends on the first try. Why? Because there are no more arrows to shoot.

Exercise:

0. Try Program Shoot.
1. Delete the static keyword and re-run. You will have to end the program from outside the program. In the Windows cmd window or on a Unix-like system, pressing CTRL + C should end the program. (Hold down the Control key, then press the C key.)
2. Make the program behave the same way as the original, without using the static keyword (use extern, or the idea of extern).
3. Why might you want to use static rather than extern? (What if you had many, many functions?)
4. BONUS. Look up another way to use the static keyword for a different behavior. For example, type "static keyword c" in your favorite internet search engine. Using static in file scope means something different from what it means in function scope.
5. BONUS. Add a function called klingons (lower-case k) to your program. Write code to tell your computer to make a static unsigned object called Klingons (upper-case K) that will keep track of how many Klingons are left. Change the program so that each time an arrow is shot, 1 is taken away from Klingons.

static

```
                    /* Program Shoot */

        #include <stdio.h>

        unsigned shoot(int asking_arrows) {
        int actual_arrows;
/*A*/       static unsigned arrow = 9;
/*B*/       char const * const onomatopoeia[] =
                { "twang!\n", "ffftp!\n" };
/*C*/       if (asking_arrows && arrow)
            actual_arrows = 1;
/*D*/       else actual_arrows = 0;
/*E*/       arrow-= actual_arrows;
/*F*/       printf(onomatopoeia[actual_arrows]);
            return arrow;
        }

        int main(void) {
/*G*/       while (shoot(!0));
            printf("\n");
/*H*/       while (shoot(!0));
            return 0;
        }

                    /* End Program Shoot */
```

PART 6

"auto **Bots, Move Out!**"

—Transformers

The auto keyword tells your computer to forget about an object. Your computer will forget when it goes out of the scope where the object is declared. The object has automatic **storage duration**. Storage duration is kind of like the *time* that an object exists. The idea is that an object can appear, disappear, and reappear at different times. The storage duration of each object is either automatic or static. You learned about static storage duration in the last chapter. If an object is not static, it is automatic.

You do not need to use the auto *keyword.* The idea behind auto is applied automatically. Nevertheless, the following is okay:

```
auto i; /* int is implied. */
```

which is the same as

```
int i; /* auto is implied. */
```

PART 7

sizeof

In Part 2, you learned that different kinds of objects take up different amounts of space. With the `sizeof` keyword, you can find out how much. The `sizeof` keyword is an *operator*. And `sizeof` is the *only* keyword in this book that is also an operator. The `sizeof` operator returns the amount of space needed to store the thing to the right of the `sizeof` operator. For example,

sizeof 'a'

returns 1, because one unit of space is required to store a character.

If your program sets aside space, `sizeof` can help you decide how much space to set aside. You can set aside space by using the `malloc` ♪ "may lock" function. If you use `malloc`, you should also use the `free` function before your program returns. The `free` function gives back the space set aside by `malloc`. Then, that space can be used by other programs or other parts of your program.

In Program Ones, the computer scans a number from the keyboard and tries to set aside space to hold that many `unsigned`'s. In other words, the computer will try to set aside enough space to hold an array of n `unsigned` objects.

Line A defines a pointer to an `unsigned` called p.

Line B uses the `malloc` function to *try* to set aside enough space to hold n `unsigned` objects. (The value of n was scanned in the line above line A.) In this case, the input of the `malloc` function is the number that was scanned, times the size of an `unsigned` object.

The malloc function returns the address of the place where it found the space—that place could be *nowhere*. In line C, the program prints the message "malloc failed!" if p points to *nowhere*. If malloc returns *nowhere*, it means that malloc did not find enough space.

Line D is inside an else block. The computer will get here only if malloc *was* able to find enough space. In line D, a for loop is used to set the values of the unsigned objects. The first time through the loop, i is zero, and p[i] is element zero in the space set aside in line B. The second time through the loop, i is one, and p[i] is element one of the same space.

Exercise:

0. Try Program Ones. When the computer asks you for a number, enter a small number, such as 1 or 2.
1. Try Program Ones again. When the computer asks you for number, enter a large number.

```
                  /* Program Ones */

         #include <malloc.h>
         #include <stdio.h>
         int main(void) {
           unsigned i, n;
           printf("Enter a number.\n");
           scanf("%u", & n);
A:;        unsigned * p;
B:         p = malloc(n * sizeof i);
C:         if (!p) printf("malloc failed!\n");
           else {
D:             for (i = 0; i < n; i++) p[i] = 1;
               for (i = 0; i < n; i++) printf("%i ", p[i]);
               free(p);
           }
           return 0;
         }

                  /* End Program Ones */
```

Sizing and Clocking:

There are limits to how much space that the `malloc` function can set aside. One limit is how much space your computer has. Another limit is the amount of space taken up by your program and by other programs. A third limit is the range of values that the input of `malloc` can handle.

The input of the `malloc` function is a number with type `size_t` 👂 "size tee," which is an unsigned type. The unsigned types are `unsigned char`, `unsigned short`, `unsigned`, and `unsigned long`. Your system defines `size_t` as one of these. You can find the greatest value allowed to be held by a `size_t` object by first giving it value 0, then subtracting one. Why does this work?

In C, the unsigned types work like a clock. When the hour hand starts out at the least value (one), then moves backwards one hour, the hand stops at the greatest value (twelve). Like the clock, when one is subtracted from an unsigned object that holds the value zero, the result is that the object holds its greatest value allowed.

You can try Program Supersize Me to see the greatest value of a `size_t` object.

```
              /* Program Supersize Me */

#include <stddef.h>   /* stddef.h defines size_t. */
#include <stdio.h>
int main(void){
    size_t s;          /* Make a size_t object named s. */
    s = 0;             /* Give s the value 0.          */
    s-= 1;             /* Subtract 1 from s.           */
    printf("%lu\n", s);/* Print s as an unsigned long. */
    return 0;
}
              /* End Program Supersize Me */
```

sizeof

PART 8

Fast, Faster, `register`

Some parts of your computer are faster than others. The `register` keyword asks your computer to handle an object as fast as possible. The computer might do this by keeping the object in a **register**. A register is a special place where your computer keeps track of something. Registers do not have addresses in the way that "normal" places in your computer have addresses. So, you can't use the & operator on a `register`'d object.

C does not tell your system exactly what to do when it sees the `register` keyword. Your system might ignore it. Your system might also make the program run slower if you use `register` where you shouldn't!

You can't be sure what `register` will do unless you know something about your system. So, you should find out how your system will treat `register` before you rely on it. If you want to try `register`, you should at least test your program with and without it.

You can use `register` by putting it in front of the type when you declare or define an object. Program Counter has an example.

Exercise:

0. Try Program Counter.
1. Delete the `register` keyword in Program Counter and try it again. On my system, the program with `register` runs about three times faster than the one without `register`. But you may get different results on your system.

register

```
#include <limits.h> /* defines ULONG_MAX */
int main(void) {
    register unsigned long i;
    for (i = 0; i < ULONG_MAX; i++);
    return 0;
}
```

/* End Program Counter */

PART 9

volatile

Sometimes, an object can be changed from outside the program. This can happen when an object gets its value from a clock, for example. Such objects are **volatile** 𝄞 "vol uh tile." If your system does not know which objects are volatile, it may take a shortcut and use old values instead of getting the new values, and using them.

You can tell your system about a volatile object by using the `volatile` keyword. For example:

```
volatile int i;
```

You should use the `volatile` keyword if your program handles volatile objects. Since each system handles volatile objects in a different way, you cannot write a program that will work properly on *any* system, but only on a *specific* system. That is why there is no example program for this chapter.

There are only three cases where you will need the `volatile` keyword. Those cases are explained by Nigel Jones in his 2001 article, "Introduction to the volatile keyword," for example. You will need to learn more about computers and programming before what he says makes sense to you. However, for the sake of completeness, the three cases are for: 1. Memory-mapped peripheral registers, 2. Global objects modified by an interrupt service routine, and 3. Global objects within a multi-threaded application.

volatile

CONCLUSION

You made it! You have learned about each of the 32 keywords of C. You have also learned about some of the operators. What else is there? A lot, actually. Among other things, C includes more operators, special names, and many, many more functions. There are also special codes that you can use to control how your system makes programs from your code.

Where do you go from here? You could try making up your own programs. You can also look at and try some of the programs on this book's website (use the shortcut, tiny.cc/cisforchildren). You could read more about C in other books or on-line. You could read about other programming languages or about programming in general. I have listed some suggested reading in the Resources and References sections.

I hope you have enjoyed this book. You can send a message to me at cisforchildren@yahoo.com. Tell me what you liked or disliked, or tell me what you would like to see in a future edition or sequel to this book.

ABOUT THE AUTHOR

D. Michael Parrish has been applying computer programming in his work and play since 1982, when, as a child, he played with a three-line BASIC program written by his mother on the Commodore VIC-20. Since then, he has acquired programming experience on a variety of platforms including the Commodore 64, the Commodore Amiga, MS DOS, Windows, UNIX / Linux, and Mac. His computer programming language experience includes BASIC, C, C++, FORTRAN, MATLAB, Pascal, and R. His status as an intermediate programmer and father of three children qualify him for the authorship of this book. He has written dozens of articles and technical reports in the fields of coastal engineering, hydrology, and computational fluid dynamics. His self portrait may be found in the Acknowledgements section.

APPENDIX

Installing and Using MinGW

MinGW can be installed by following the instructions at http://mingw.org/wiki/Getting_Started. Install MinGW in the default location (something like C:\MinGW).

Copy the programs of this book into C:\MinGW\bin. If you want to type them in yourself, you can use a text editor such as Notepad, and save to C:\MinGW\.

To compile a program, open the command line editor (in Windows 95 through Windows 8, use the Start menu to run the program cmd) and enter:

```
C:
cd \
cd MinGW\bin
gcc programName.c -std=c89
```

This assumes that MinGW is installed on the C drive. The compiler will produce an executable file called a.exe. To run the newly compiled program, enter a. You can also name the output of the compiler, like this:

```
gcc programName.c -o programName.exe
```

The gcc compiler will "complain" if you are breaking any rules of the C language. It will usually tell you where in your source code the problems are. This will come in the form of two numbers: a line number and a column number.

GLOSSARY

. dot operator. used to tell about a member of a structure or union.

. decimal point. used when forming floating point numbers.

\n when found between single or double quotes, this sequence means new-line.

(open parenthesis. used with) to group items together.

) close parenthesis. used with (to group items together.

[open bracket. used with] to tell about items in an array.

] close bracket. used with [to tell about items in an array.

; semicolon. marks the end of a statement.

{ open brace. used to tell where a block begins.

} close brace. used to tell where a block ends.

++ increment operator. used to add one to an integer.

& address operator. used to return the address of an object.

* indirection operator, "star." used to tell about a pointer type.

* multiplication operator. used to return the product of two numbers.

/* used at the beginning of a comment.

*/ used at the end of a comment.

+ addition operator. used to return the sum of two numbers.

- subtraction operator. used to return the difference between two numbers.

! logical negation operator. meaning *not*.

/ division operator. used to return the quotient of two numbers.

% modulus operator. used to return the remainder of division.

< less than operator. used to test if one number is less than another.

> greater than operator. used to test if one number is greater than another.

☺ smile. This symbol is not used in C.

<= less than or equal to operator. used to test if one number is *not* greater than another.

\>= greater than or equal to operator. used to test if one number is *not* less than another.

== equality operator. used to test if one number is equal to another.

!= inequality operator. used to test if one number is not equal to another.

&& logical *and* operator. used to test if two things are true.

: colon. used to make a label.

= assignment operator. used to tell an object what value to hold.

+= addition assignment operator. used to add to an object.

-= subtraction assignment operator. used to subtract from an object.

, comma. used to separate items in a list.

used to include headers.

-2,147,483,647: A `long` can hold values as low as this number.

-32,767: An `int` can hold values as low as this number.

-127: A `signed char` can hold values down to this number.

0: Number at which C begins counting. Lowest possible element number for an array.

0.25: Number of dollars I paid my children to review an early draft of this book.

0.333333: Almost one-third.

⅓: Portion of a day most people sleep.

½: Average odds.

1: The minimum size for an object. The size of a character object.

⅝: The slope of the graph of degrees Fahrenheit versus degrees Celsius.

2.71828182845904590: Euler's number.

3: The grade level at which you should be able to read this book. Approximate of the ratio of a circle's circumference to its diameter.

3.1415926535897932: distance around a circle divided by the distance across a circle—almost.

4: Number of parts in a function.

5: According to King Arthur (see the 1975 film *Monty Python and the Holy Grail*), the number that comes after two.

6: 42 ÷ 7

7: 42 ÷ 6

8: The size of a `double` on many systems.

9: Number of fingers Frodo was left with after a fight with Gollum.

10: The number of fingers on two hands. The Queen of Hearts holds this value in many card games.

12: One dozen. The Number of Apostles. The number of Tribes of Israel.

14: Two times seven.

20: a score.

21: A card game in which the players try to get a sum of 21.

25: Number of cents in a quarter of a dollar.

31: Number of characters that your system will see in the names you make.

32: The number of keywords in C89.

39: Number of lashes Jesus received before his crucifixion.

40: Number of columns on the screen of the Commodore 64.

42: What is six times seven? Or, the answer to the question of life, the universe, and everything (Adams). Or, both!

50: A Skitty Pokemon has this many HP.

100: number of cents in a dollar.

127: A `char` can hold values up to this number.

132: standard number of characters on a wide-carriage printer.

153: Number of fish caught by Peter, Thomas, Nathanael, James, John, and two Disciples.

255: An `unsigned char` can hold values up to this number.

2000: Approximate year I read *Just Enough Unix*.

2014: The year of our Lord that this book was published.

32767: An `int` is guaranteed to hold numbers up to this value.

32,768: 2^{16}. On some systems, this value is too large to be held by an `int`.

65,535: An `unsigned` or `unsigned short` can hold values up to this number.

2,147,483,647: A `long` can hold values as great as this number.

3,011,070,705: one of many ten-digit numbers whose value can be held by a `double`.

4,294,967,295: An `unsigned long` can hold values up to this number.

301,107,070,500,000,000,000,000 about equal to one half of a **mole**, using the number suggested by R. F. Fox and T. P. Hill in their 2007 article in *American Scientist* (vol. 95, pp 104-107), "An exact value for Avogadro's number."

address: something that tells where some part of your program is.

array: a group of objects of the same type. Each item in the group is a neighbor of one or two other items in the group.

assignment statement: a statement having an equals sign (=) that tells what value an object should hold.

backslash: the symbol \

BASIC: a computer programming language designed for beginners; created at Dartmouth College by John Kemey, Thomas Kurtz, and their students.

block scope: the part of a program that can be "seen" from inside a **block** (see Figure 3).

block: part of a program found between braces {}.

blow up: to stop working.

braces: the symbols {}

brackets: the symbols []

C: the subject of this book; a computer programming language designed at Bell Labs by Brian Kernighan and Dennis Ritchie.

C++: a computer programming language that includes almost all of C, but is different in some important ways; developed by Bjarne Stroustrup at Bell Labs.

character: 1. a letter, digit, punctuation mark, or symbol used in writing. 2. an object that holds a character.

close brace: the symbol }

comment: part of a program ignored by the computer. Comments are found between the symbols /* and */.

compiler: a program that reads a computer programming language and writes instructions for your computer called machine code.

controversial: having opposite responses depending on who is responding.

crash: to stop working.

declare: to tell the computer that an object exists, and to tell its type.

def: slang word meaning "excellent."

define: to tell what value an object should hold.

digit: one of the characters 0, 1, 2, 3, 4, 5, 6, 7, 8, or 9.

dot operator: the symbol . (period), used to tell about a member of a structure or union.

double quotes: the symbol " " or "

element: one item in an array.

enumerated 𝔇 "ee new mer ray Ted:" numbered.

expression: something that returns a value.

file scope: the part of a program that can be "seen" anywhere in the program (see Figure 3).

floating point number: a kind of number that could be an integer or a number in between two integers.

format 👂 "for mat:" the way numbers, characters, or strings are printed, such as with spaces in front, or with a new line at the end.

FORTRAN: a computer programming language developed at IBM by John Backus and others.

`free`: a function that gives back the space set aside by `malloc`.

function 👂 "funk shun:" part of a program that tells the computer what to do, and *in what order*. Functions have four parts: a name, input, a process, and output.

function definition: tells the return type, name, input, and process of a function.

function prototype scope: the part of a program that can be seen only from inside a **function prototype** (see Figure 3).

function scope: the part of a program that can be "seen" from inside a function (see Figure 3).

garbage: any value at all, and no value in particular.

header: part of a program kept outside and ahead of another part.

implied 👂 "imp lied:" unsaid or unwritten, but present.

integer: one of the numbers 0, 1, -1, 2, -2, 3, -3 . . .

integral 👂 "int egg roll:" having to do with integers.

jump: to skip over one or more statements.

label: a name that goes at the beginning of a statement. You can use a `goto` statement to jump to a statement that has a label.

`limits.h`: C header that has the definition of the ranges of `int`, `char`, and the other types.

linkage: 👂 "link age:" having to do with what objects can be seen, and from where.

loop: part of a program that runs more than once.

machine code: your computer's "native" language.

`main`: function where a program starts. Every C program must have `main`.

`malloc` 👂 "may lock:" a function that tells the computer to set aside space.

maximum: the biggest or greatest something can be.

member: one part of a structure or union; a trait.

mole: an amount of something that can be counted, about 301,107,070,500,000,000,000,000 of them.

minimum: the smallest or least something can be.

name: a sequence of characters used to refer to an object, function, or other part of your program.

nested loop: a loop inside a loop.

new-line: 1. a character that tells the computer to start a new line during output. 2. the sequence \n

null character: a special character that can mean the end of a string, empty, nothing, and the like.

null statement: a statement meaning "do nothing."

onomatopoeia 𝔇 "on no ma toe pee yuh:" words that sound like what they mean.

open brace: the symbol {

parentheses 𝔇 "puh ren thuh seas:" the symbols ( )

parenthesis 𝔇 "puh ren thuh siss:" the symbol) or (

pointer: an address. A pointer tells where a part of your program is.

pound sign: the symbol #

program: directions or instructions for your computer.

prototype 𝔇 "pro toe type:" similar to object declarations, function prototypes tell the computer that a function exists, what the return type is, and what the inputs are.

range: the space between boundaries or limits.

register: A special place where your computer keeps track of something. Registers do not have addresses in the way that "normal" places in your computer have addresses.

return type: the type returned by a function or other operation.

return: to give back a value or address.

run: to do what a program says to do.

safe: to do things in ways that avoid crashes.

scanf: function that gets characters from your keyboard and puts them in your computer.

scope: having to do with what can be "seen" from different parts of a program.

semicolon: the punctuation mark ;

single quote: the symbol ' ' or '

size_t 𝔇 "size tee:" an unsigned type; the type returned by sizeof.

square brackets: brackets

standard output: a place where the computer sends information, such as the screen.

star: the symbol * called "asterisk" in most other books.

`stddef.h`: header that has the definition of `size_t`.

`stdio.h`: header that has the definitions of `printf` and `scanf`.

`string.h`: header that has the definition of `strncpy`.

storage duration: The time or place when or where that an object exists. Objects can appear, disappear, and reappear at different places.

string: one or more characters in a row.

structure 𝔇 "struck sure:" a group of objects. Each object in a structure is called a **member**.

system: the combination of a computer, operating system, and compiler.

this: If you need to look up the word "this," please put this book back on the shelf. However, please try again when your reading level in English is up to grade two or three.

type: another word for *kind*, as in, "What kind of flower are you?"

type: symbols, or kinds of symbols used in printing.

type: to touch keys on a keyboard.

underscore: the symbol _

union 𝔇 "yoon yun:" like a structure, except that the members of a union are stored in the same space, whereas the members of a structure are each stored in their own space.

value: a number that goes with an object or constant.

GLOSSARY OF KEYWORDS

The Part and Chapter where each keyword first appears are shown like this: [part][chapter].

auto: keyword that tells the computer to forget about an object when the computer goes out of the scope where that object is **declared**. [6][]

break: keyword that tells the computer to jump to the next statement after a loop. [3][4]

case: keyword that tells what value the computer should try to match to the object given using the switch statement. [3][4]

char ℘ "care" or "char:" a keyword that tells about a character object. [2][1], see also [4][1]

char []: C code for character array. [2][1]

const: keyword that tells about an object that should not be changed by code that you write. [5][]

continue: keyword that tells the computer to jump to the beginning of a loop. [3][7]

default: keyword used in a switch statement. Statements that are part of a default case will be run, no matter what value is held by the object given in the switch statement. [3][4]

do: keyword that tells computer to do a do loop. [3][3]

double: keyword that tells the computer to make a floating point number that can hold at least 10 digits. [4][0]

else: keyword that tells what to do. [3][1]

enum: keyword that tells about an enumerated type. [4][0]

extern: keyword that tells that an object is in file scope. [5][0]

float: keyword that tells the computer to make a floating point number that can hold at least 6 digits. [4][0]

`for:` keyword that tells the computer to do a for loop. [3][6]

`goto:` keyword that tells the computer to jump to a labeled statement. [3][5]

`if:` keyword that tells the computer to do a statement only if a certain test is true. [3][0]

`int:` keyword used to tell about a number that can hold integer values from -32,767 to 32,767. [0][2]

`long:` keyword used to tell about a number that can hold integer values from -2,147,483,647 to 2,147,483,647. [4][1] see also [4][0]

`register:` keyword that tells the computer to work with an object as fast as possible. [8][]

`return:` keyword that tells the computer to jump out of a function and, possibly, give back a certain value. [0][4]

`short:` keyword used to tell about a number that can hold integer values from -32,767 to 32,767. [4][1]

`signed:` keyword that tells about an integral object that can hold both negative and positive values. [4][1]

`sizeof:` keyword that returns the size of the object to the right. [7][]

`static:` keyword that tells the computer to remember an object's value when it goes to a different scope. There is another way to use static that is not covered by this book. [5][1]

`struct:` keyword that tells about a structure, a group of objects held together. [4][2]

`switch:` keyword that tells what object to look at while going through cases. [3][4]

`typedef:` keyword used to make a nickname for a type that you make. [4][4]

`union:` keyword that tells about a group of objects that are kept in the same place. [4][3]

`unsigned:` keyword that tells that an integer will not have values less than zero. Used by itself, an integer that can hold values from 0 to 65,535. [4][1]

`void:` keyword that means nothing, or nothing in particular. [0][0]

`volatile` 𝄞 "vol uh tile:" keyword that tells about an object whose value may change at any time, for reasons that are not explained by the code. [9][]

`while:` keyword used to tell the computer to do a while loop. This keyword is also used at the end of a do loop. [3][2]

RESOURCES

Websites:

cprogramming.com
flash-gordon.me.uk/ansi.c.txt
gcc.gnu.org
mingw.org
stackoverflow.com

Articles and Books:

Brodie, Leo. *Thinking Forth: A Language and Philosophy for Solving Problems.* Thinking Forth Project, 2004. At: http://thinking-forth.sourceforge.net/

Gookin, Dan. *C All-in-One Desk Reference for Dummies.* Wiley, 2004. ISBN: 978-0-7645-7069-8.

Hopkins, Martin E. "A Case for the GOTO," *Proceedings of the ACM Annual Conference.* ACM, 1972. doi:10.1145/800194.805860

International Organization for Standardization and International Electrotechnical Commission. ISO/IEC 9899:2011 Information technology—Programming languages—C. 2011. http://webstore.ansi.org/RecordDetail.aspx?sku= ISO%2FIEC+9899%3A2011

Kernighan, Brian W. and Dennis M. Ritchie. *The C Programming Language,* 2nd ed. Prentice Hall, 1988.

Plauger, P.J. *The C Standard Library.* Prentice Hall, 1992.

REFERENCES

Adams, Douglas. *The Hitchhiker's Guide to the Galaxy*. Pan Books, 1979

Berenstain, Stan and Jan. *Inside, Outside, Upside Down*. Random House, 1968.

Brooks, Mel, Thomas Meehan, and Ronny Graham. *Spaceballs*. Film. Directed by Mel Brooks. Brooksfilms and MGM, 1987.

Carroll, Lewis. *Through the Looking-Glass and What Alice Found There*. MacMillan, 1872.

Goldman, William. *The Princess Bride*. Film. Directed by Rob Reiner. Act III Communications; Buttercup Films, Ltd.; The Princess Bride, Ltd. 1987.

Heinecke, Kurt. *The Veggie Tales Theme*. Big Idea Entertainment, LLC, 1993.

Jones, Nigel. "Introduction to the volatile keyword." 2001. On-line at: http://www.embedded.com/electronics-blogs/beginner-s-corner/4023801/Introduction-to-the-Volatile-Keyword. accessed 11 July 2013

Lerner, Alan Jay and Bernard Shaw. *My Fair Lady*. Film. Directed by George Cukor. Warner Bros, 1964.

Lucas, George. *Star Wars*. Film. Directed by George Lucas. Lucasfilm, Twentieth Century Fox Film Corporation, 1977

Parmenides of Elea. Greek Philosopher.

Petersen, Wolfgang and Herman Weigel. *The Neverending Story*. Film. Directed by Wolfgang Petersen. Warner Bros, 1984.

Smith, Robert Paul and James J. Spanfeller. *Where Did You Go? Out. What Did You Do? Nothing*. W.W. Norton & Co., 1957.

Transformers. Television Program. Sunbow Productions, Marvel Productions, and Hasbro, 1984